Boscast

The coast is exceedingly exposed and dangerous,
to approach. The ground-swell, which sometim
terrific. The sea rises like mountains and sweeps
tect the harbour's mouth, covering the loftiest crags with foam and spray.

The History of the Deanery of Trigg Minor 1873

The creation of a harbour at Boscastle in the rather unlikely setting of a deep ravine in a formidable section of one of Britain's most dangerous coastlines, was 'a marvellous instance of what may be accomplished by the right sort of enterprise'.

Records show that in 1337 Boscastle became one of a string of tiny fishing ports farmed out by the Duchy of Cornwall's havener, for the payment of 20/- per year. But no quay of any consequence appears to have been erected before the mid sixteenth century.

In 1547 the Chantries Act Commissioners had recommended that the local stipendiary priests should donate part of their income for the upkeep of the quay as a gracious and merciful act of charity. Two years later the church of St Thomas in Launceston contributed money to the damaged quay and other money was raised by subscription. However, the repaired early structure was not substantial enough to withstand the battering of the Atlantic elements, and quay construction appears to have taken place again in 1584. This was publicly funded, with many local people contributing some of the labour free of charge. But the harbour was an integral part of the manor, and the Lord of the Manor (in this case Sir Richard Grenville, Sheriff of Cornwall), who was in receipt of dues, was responsible for the upkeep.

The present quay and harbour wall were constructed by Cotton Amy Esq in 1740, while the outer breakwater on the northern side was added around 1820. But despite these measures the swell continued to penetrate into the inner harbour and cause problems for shipping in certain weather conditions. This photograph was taken in the 1890s.

Maritime Activity

The little harbour is really a reft in the rocks, or a romantic creek . . . but it is a place of great safety and use for shipping of the smaller class. It is one of the prettiest sights imaginable to . . . see a vessel towed in by a boat of sturdy rowers, her sails still spread, and moving gracefully like a thing of life, until the headland is taken. Hawsers as big as your body are here called into use, and soon the little bark lies snug and safe within the tortuous windings of the creek . . . .

A Guide to North Cornwall W. L. POWELL 1884

Boscastle was the busy scene of maritime activity in the nineteenth and early twentieth centuries, when cargo vessels traded regularly with South Wales, Bristol, Gloucester, Appledore and other places, and the port had its own small fishing fleet. However, entering and leaving the harbour was never easy, even in calm conditions, and hobblers played an essential part. Traditionally

hobblers (or hovellers) were unlicensed pilots or boatmen who went out in gigs or small rowing boats to tow sailing vessels in and out of the north Cornish ports, where the hazards of prevailing winds and currents, and constricted entrances, called for specialist local knowledge.

When a ship wanted to enter harbour, it was usual to drop anchor and furl her sails beyond the harbour limits. Then the hobbling boat would take her in tow. Having achieved entry to the curving, constricted channel, it was a case of highly controlled manoeuvring, for getting vessels in and out of port involved a variety of painstaking techniques. These included the use of lines, buoys, anchors and warps to blocks and rings secured to the cliffs, and tow horses. Sometimes there was an elaborate system of strategically positioned lines and anchors creating a pulley system, with villagers supplying the muscle power. The situation of having to get around tight corners limited the size of vessels able to use the harbour.

Shipping at Boscastle

Loading and unloading

Vessels were usually loaded and unloaded alongside the quay. However, in very poor weather conditions it was safer for them to be made fast to permanent ground moorings and steadied by giant warps fore and aft in the inner harbour, for this reduced the friction and stress on the superstructure and the dangers of parting their timbers. In this situation loading and discharging of cargoes took place over the side at low tide, using packhorses, mules and horse-drawn carts in the traditional manner.

The gigantic hawsers

Boscastle was renowned for its gigantic hawsers (anchor cables), for the ropes and lines usually employed elsewhere would have been useless here. Large supplies were always kept in readiness on the quaysides, neatly looped over stout, stumpy bollards. In the mid nineteenth century, which was the port's heyday, it was remarked that hawsers like these were used on the Thames to tow the stately East Indiamen. At this time Boscastle was a thriving centre of maritime commerce and industry, serving Launceston and a wide agricultural hinterland, supporting some mining, quarrying and china clay activities. There were lime kilns, mills powered by water wheels, a malting house, smithy and pottery near the head of the creek, and the quaysides were lined with warehouses, workshops, shipyards, timberyards and all the appliances of a busy trading port.

Centre of maritime commerce and industry

Warping in a trading ketch. This dramatic portrayal of Boscastle harbour shows the pulley system in action, with a team of men working the enormous hawsers, for which Boscastle was renowned, above the jetty on the left.

Seafarers' welfare

Establishments for the welfare of seafarers included a Coastguard Station, equipped with a Board of Trade Life Saving Apparatus, and a branch of the Shipwrecked Fishermen and Mariners' Benevolent Society.

In its nineteenth-century heyday, the energetic walker on the towering heights above the constricted little harbour would have seen an array of masts and rigging, for at that time a fleet of ketches, smacks, sloops and small wooden schooners were operating in and out of the port, catering for the needs of a wide rural area extending to Launceston and the moors.

Ship construction

Some vessels had been constructed here, as well as at Port Isaac and Port Gaverne in previous centuries, and about eight ships were built in Boscastle during the nineteenth century.

Trade

In the late nineteenth century and the early twentieth century, trade was mostly with Bristol, Gloucester and South Wales. The *Lively* and the *Bedoe* of Appledore brought in coal, manure and iron, but this trade had fallen away by about 1930, and after the Second World War things became rather quiet around the harbourside, apart from the occasional appearance of a yacht seeking shelter from a storm.

Boscastle harbour looking eastwards to the head of the creek, 1898.

The Toun of Boscastelle lyith apon the Brow of a rokky Hille by South Est, and so goith doun by length to the Northe toward the Se, but not even ful hard to it . . . the Bleke Northern Se is not there of Nature favorable.

LELAND

The 1500s

The 1700s

John Leland saw this as a hostile environment in the sixteenth century, but 250 years later the literary traveller W. G. Maton, responded in a very different way, putting it neatly in its topographical context:

'From Tintagel we proceed over a rocky road to Boscastle, a village in a highly romantic situation. The cottages are all in a deep valley washed by a small inlet of the sea, whilst fine mountainous eminences crowd round them on all sides, cut by craggy gaps, and clad with brushwood.'

The 1800s

Perhaps he might be regarded as an early tourist, who came here for pleasure, relating to the people and the place.

Thomas Hardy, in the late nineteenth century, had a more sombre perception of its charms, and this provided a powerful atmospheric background for his novel *A Pair of Blue Eyes*.

Today

Today much of the land in and around the picturesque harbour and village is owned by the National Trust, including the commanding cliffs of Penally Point and Willapark, which guard the sinuous harbour entrance. Forrabury Common, high above the village, and divided into anciently established 'stitchmeal' cultivation plots, and large areas of woodland and meadow in the lovely Valency Valley are also in the care of the Trust.

A traveller and his donkey pictured near the harbour entrance in 1905.

Boscastle is as picturesque and as romantic as can be desired, a perfectly enchanting spot.

Guide to North Cornwall

W. L. POWELL 1884

Geological formations

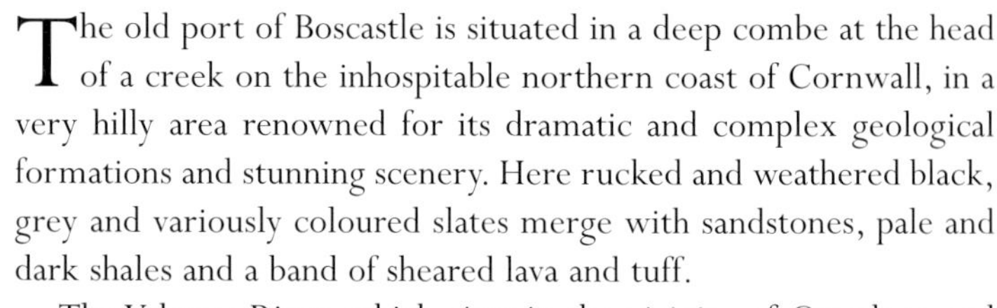

The old port of Boscastle is situated in a deep combe at the head of a creek on the inhospitable northern coast of Cornwall, in a very hilly area renowned for its dramatic and complex geological formations and stunning scenery. Here rucked and weathered black, grey and variously coloured slates merge with sandstones, pale and dark shales and a band of sheared lava and tuff.

The Valency River, which rises in the vicinity of Otterham and Marshgate, makes its way westwards, gathering tributaries from the steeply enfolded hills before uniting with the shorter River Jordan, just above the head of the creek. The romantic, steep sided valley of the Valency creates a protective environment, where trees and flowers proliferate and wildlife abounds. The waters ripple and dance their way through dappled glens, before reaching the confines of the harbour, where lofty hills cast sombre shadows across the dramatic terrain. This energy now runs free, but there was a time when every little stream was harnessed by watermills. The sheltered, flowery and luxuriant river valleys contrast sharply with the starkly windswept, high and undulating cliffs of the Atlantic seaboard.

Footbridge over the Valency River.

Children playing by the bridge over the Valency in 1905, and the rising rugged terrain beyond.

Boscastle harbour is actually the drowned mouth of the incised river valley, bordered by steep, craggy slopes, in strongly folded slates and sandstones of the Crackington Formation. Here the united rivers widen into a winding, tidal inlet, flowing into the sea beneath Penally Point. This headland is pierced by a cave, which is exposed for an hour or so at low water, but can become a spectacular blowhole when strong waves are driven through a crevice from the seaward side. It will eventually erode to form an outlying slate stack, like the elevated little island of Meachard lying just offshore.

The island of Meachard and the coastal craggy slate slopes that are so characteristic of this area.

Earthworks ancient and modern

A scattering of tumuli, long barrows, ancient encampments and other earthworks throughout this area, bear witness to human occupations from very early times, while a proliferation of disused pits and quarries tell a tale of human endeavour in a pastoral landscape where the agricultural and excavational industries were made viable by the old port. By 1873 the mining and quarrying activities had ceased and cultivation of the soil was the only land-based industry.

The sparsely populated area between the moors and the sea can become rather bleak in the winter, but there have been on-going climatic changes since those early tribes first colonised the region, and successfully gleaned a livlihood from the environment. From the steeply rising hinterland there are wonderful views of the deep valleys and dramatic coastline, with the bold mass of Lundy Island rising in the distance.

When Lundy is high, it will be dry,
When Lundy is plain, it will rain,
When Lundy is low, it will be snow.

The Parishes of Forrabury and Minster

Boscastle harbour falls within the parish of Forrabury (formerly known as *Ferebyri* or *Forbury*), whereas most of the ancient town is situated in the parish of Minster (formerly known as *Talcarn*). The history of these parishes is closely interlinked, for both were included within the Honour, Manor and Fee of Worthevale and the Manor of Botreaux Castle. The parish of Forrabury, adjoining the parishes of Trevalga and Minster, and bounded on the north by the Atlantic Ocean, is one of the smallest parishes in the county. The parish of Minster, adjoined by this parish and a small section of seacoast, is bounded by the parishes of St Juliot, Lesnewth, Davidstow, Lanteglos, St Teath, Advent, Tintagel and Trevalga.

For centuries this region was the domain of the ancient and celebrated de Bottreaux family, but by the mid nineteenth century, Thomas Rickard Avery had become Lord of the Manor, with William Sloggatt Esq and William Roseveare being acknowledged as the chief landowners. By the end of that century the Hellyar, Roseveare, Hawker and Spry families had emerged as the principal landowners.

Botreaux Castle

Boscastle derives its name from Botreaux Castle, which was one of the old baronial residences of the ancient Norman French family of Botreaux, or as John Norden, the Elizabethan historian rather more engagingly put it, 'The name attributed first vnto the Castle only, but as the towne increased it retayned only the name of the Castle as it doth this daye.' The old town of *Botreaux Castle* is thought to have had a population of 181 in 1377.

One of the coats-of-arms of the Botreaux family.

The castle was situated on the sharp spur of a hill at the junction of two valleys, in a place known as Jordans. By 1873 the site was occupied by buildings and gardens, but the outer and inner walls on the lower, northern side were still distinguishable. The ancient structure was of circular form, and at that time marked by mounds of rubbish, from which ashlar stones had been removed for building purposes. Although its situation was commanding from one side, its effectiveness as a fortress was questionable, as it was dominated by higher ground on the other three sides. The castle incorporated a prison for both sexes but its notoriety outlasted its fabric and Botreaux Castle is thought to have fallen into decay in the reign of Henry VI, when the heiress of the family married Lord Hungerford, whose possessions lay at a considerable distance from here.

Welltown

This manor house in the parish of Forrabury was built by the Tinck family. When yeoman John Tinck died, he left two-thirds of it to his elder son John, and the remaining third to his younger son Baldwin. John's decision to convey his share to William Cotton Esq of Exeter led to quarrels and contentions between Baldwin and William Cotton, which resulted in the house being partitioned by a deed dated 28 February 1610. The deed made mention of the hall, the parlour, three chambers over the parlour, and the buttery.

The Botreaux (or Boterell) family

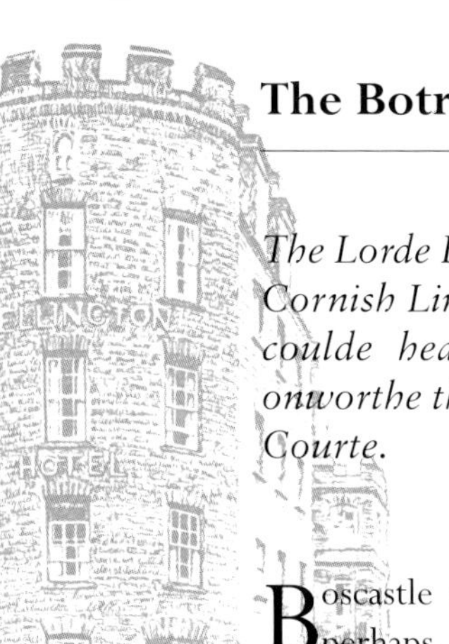

The turreted Wellington Hotel belies the fact that no trace remains of the original castle from which Boscastle takes its name.

The Lorde Botreaux was Lord of this Toun, a man of an old Cornish Linage, and had a Maner Place, a Thing, as far as I coulde heare, of smaul Reputation, as it is now, far onworthe the name of a Castel. The People ther caulle it the Courte.

JOHN LELAND 1534–43

Boscastle still retains the air of its feudal past, perpetuated, perhaps, by the turreting of the Wellington Hotel in the late nineteenth century. The old town, clustered around the southern and western sides of the castle, would have been built by the retainers and vassals of the Lord, and others who sought his protection.

In 1312 William, son of William de Botereus, had a charter dated 16 August granting to him and his heirs for ever, a weekly market and a three-day weekly fair on the eve, the day and the morrow of St James the Apostle, providing it had no detrimental effect on neighbouring markets and fairs. The fairs subsequently became two day events and the market eventually dwindled away. The market house was demolished around 1870.

William Botreaux and his younger brother, Reginald, were both among the rebels in conflict with Henry III. In 1368, William de Botreaux, who was the eighth to carry that name, was created a baron.

William, Lord Botreaux, the last of the family, was killed at the second battle of St Albans in 1461, leaving an only daughter, who married Sir Robert Hungerford. Their only child, Mary, was deemed at that time to be the richest heiress that ever lived, being 'seized in her own right of upwards of a hundred manors in different counties'. Her husband, who was also Marquis of Hastings, sold Botreaux Castle to John Hender esq. The estate passed to the Cotton family, and then to William Amy of Tintagel in the early eighteenth century.

William Amy's grand-daughter married Jonathan Phillips. Grace Amy and Ann Amy, daughters of Cotton Amy, subsequently became tenants in common. The younger sister, Ann, 'had the misfortune to be a lunatic', so Sir Jonathan managed the property on her behalf.

When he died in 1799, management of the estate passed to the Revd John Kingdon of Bridgerule and the Revd John Kingdon, Junior, who were Ann's next of kin. The estate encountered further difficulties when Richard Benoke experienced cash-flow problems and was obliged to mortgage his interest, which led to the estate coming into the possession of various people, including Thomas Rickard Avery, who did much to improve the place, and the Hellyars.

The Botreaux family had come to an end for the lack of an heir. Then by a succession of marriages the title of Baron Botreaux became one of the minor titles of the fourth and last Marquis of Hastings. The title lapsed on his death in 1868, but was revived in 1871, in favour of the Countess of Loudown.

The ship rode down with courses free,
The daughter of a distant sea,
Her sheet was loose, her anchor stored
The merry Bottreaux bells on board.

According to legend, the ship carrying the precious bells of Bottreaux, which were cast to rival the bells of Tintagel, was wrecked in a sudden storm off the headland of Willapark. The captain, a native of Tintagel, was the only crew member to survive and to this day some claim to hear the sunken bells ringing in a storm.

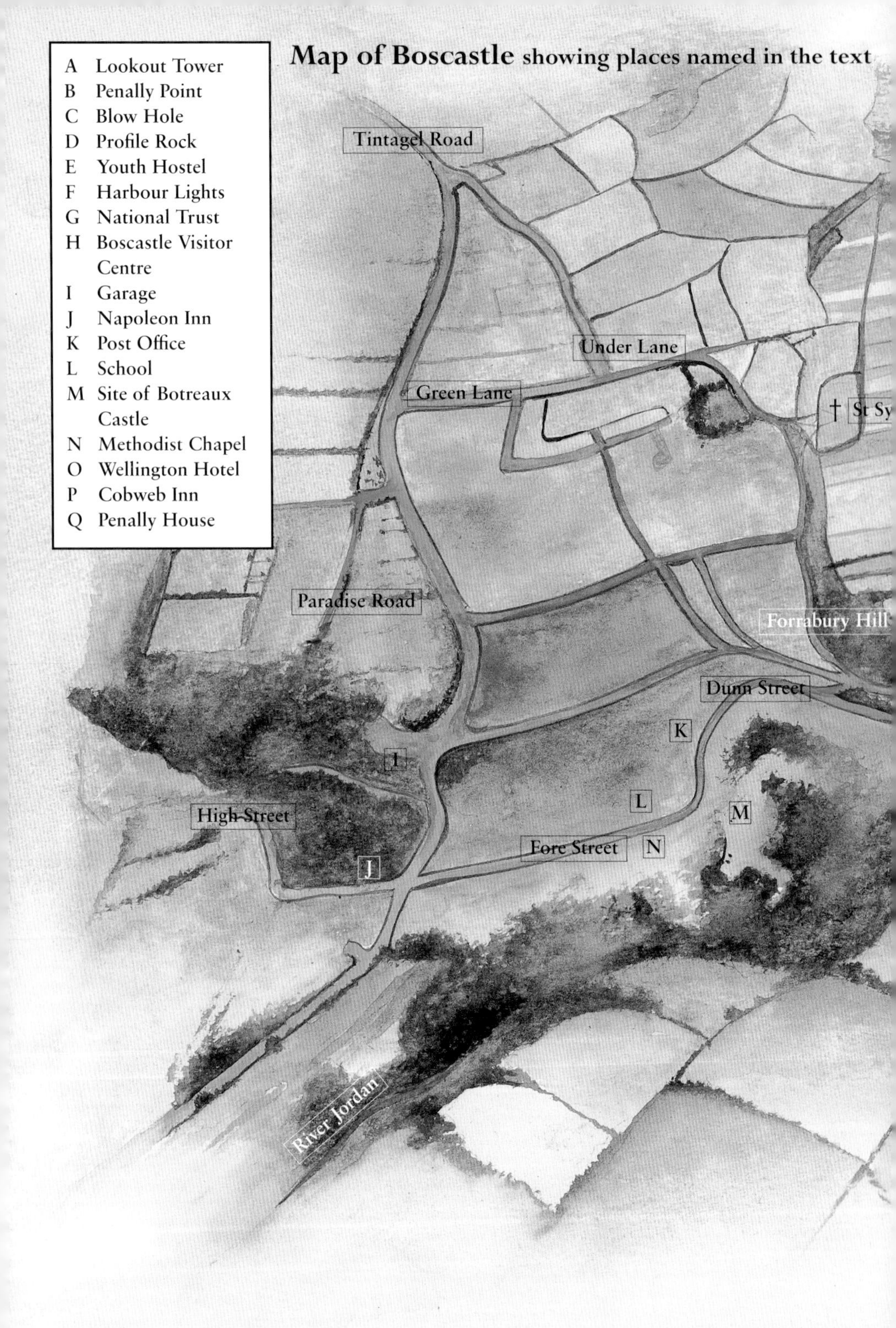
Map of Boscastle showing places named in the text
A Lookout Tower
B Penally Point
C Blow Hole
D Profile Rock
E Youth Hostel
F Harbour Lights
G National Trust
H Boscastle Visitor Centre
I Garage
J Napoleon Inn
K Post Office
L School
M Site of Botreaux Castle
N Methodist Chapel
O Wellington Hotel
P Cobweb Inn
Q Penally House
Tintagel Road
Under Lane
Green Lane
Paradise Road
Forrabury Hill
Dunn Street
K
I
L
M
High Street
Fore Street
N
J
River Jordan

A
Meachard
N
Willapark
D
B
C
Harbour
bury Common
an's
E
F
G
New Road
Old Mill Road
Old Road
O
H
P
Valency River
Green Cut
Q
Valency Valley
Walk

Mercantile trade

Between 1820 and 1870 records state that corn (barley, oats for cattle and wheat for general purposes), malt, slate, china clay and china stone, manganese and bark were exported. However, the quarries ceased working a few years later. Imports included wines, beers and spirits, hardware such as bricks and pottery, groceries, limestone, timber, draining tiles, manures and corn for agricultural use. The establishment of a brewery at Redruth boosted trade for Boscastle. The port did very well with timber imported by Mr Avery, who had also created a malting business. After his death both businesses ceased to be viable on account of the hefty dues demanded of those who sought to take them over. So the trade went to the rival ports of Padstow and Bude, where minimal or no dues were levied.

In the 1860s the vast quantities of iron ore being brought from Trebursye, two miles from Launceston, boosted the port of Boscastle. There was great excitement when Cornwall's first traction engine arrived at Trebursye, for the purpose of taking ores to Boscastle and returning with coal. The locomotive completed its first haul to Boscastle in April 1862, despite delays, but the inadequate roads and repeated breakdowns, not to mention its ability to make horses bolt and set things on fire, gave it a questionable reputation.

Lively *of Bideford, 'whip' rigged for discharging cargo into waiting wagons.*

Most of the cargoes handled here were of less than 100 tons.

In 1858, 51 tons of magnetic iron ore and manganese mills were operating in premises near the harbour. The nearby mines of *Wheal Beeny* and *North Wheal Rusey* in the parish of St Juliot, producing silver and lead, also provided employment for local people. Strong teams of horses, mostly kept in harbourside stables, hauled the heavy loads up the steep gradients. The Green Cut was created around the lower slopes of Penally Hill to the harbour, and the New Road was built in 1886 to lessen the problems of the steep gradients.

The fertilizer trade

While I am writing this, a string of sand-loaded carts are passing up a steep road before my windows. This incline is certainly near a mile in length; it has been well and skilfully made by the Boscastleites, but it needs three horses to drag about a cubic yard-and-a half of sea-sand up the hill. So highly valued is this sand that it is frequently drawn from the sea-shore up apparently impossible inclines, and over such rough roads that none but the active little Cornish cart horses could surmount. And in places where the cliffs are so steep that only pathways exist, they carry the sand from the shore to the top of the cliffs in bags on the backs of donkeys, from whence it is carted on to the land.

THE WEST BRITON 1 November, 1876

Boscastle built up a trade in fertilizers, and by the 1870s several manure and lime merchants were operating from here. Imported limestone would be burnt in quayside kilns, mixed with layers of culm (coal), to produce quicklime and lime ash for agricultural purposes. The lime kiln was a focal point of work-a-day local life, where folk converged in an agreeably warm situation, conducive to a yarn and a drink or two. However, quicklime is a highly dangerous substance, and some appalling accidents occurred at limekilns around the coast.

Sea sand and lime were much in demand by inland farmers, to lighten heavy soils and reduce acidity. A thirteenth-century charter had given Cornishmen permission to extract sea sand from the beaches, and many farm leases required tenants to replenish the soil with manure and other nutrients before ploughing. Large quantities of sea sand, with some fish waste and seaweed, were used to improve impoverished soil on the more barren areas of Bodmin Moor.

The Lively *of Bideford alongside the quay in 1902.*

The Fishing Industry

The nerve centre of Boscastle in 1898, with an array of mercantile buildings, the bridge over the Valency, and a mill to the right of the white cottages.

Kelly's Directory of 1889 tells us that 'attempts have been made to establish a pilchard fishery' here. Although Boscastle, with its tortuous channel cut out of the towering hills by the little Valency River, may seem a rather unlikely environment to support a fishing industry, the place had its own seine in the early part of the nineteenth century, when capacious fish cellars and a large salt-house were situated on the quayside. These buildings, along with the boats, tackle and materials of the Boscastle Seine were put up for sale in 1811, and nine years later the buildings were back on the market, and advertised as being suitable for conversion into workmen's dwellings, workshops or storehouses for the mercantile trade.

If the constricted harbour had its drawbacks, it also had its advantages, for when large quantities of sprats entered the channel, pursued by mackerel, the fishermen placed a net across the harbour entrance and caught them on the ebbing tide. In 1884 lobsters and prawns were said to have been very plentiful here.

The Old Bakehouse, High Street, Boscastle.

The Seal Trade

During the summer a number of seals are taken by the Boscastle fishermen. The coast is everywhere undermined by deep caverns, which, when the sea is smooth, the fishermen enter in their boats and explore with torches. The seals, which are fond of lying on ledges in these gloomy retreats, are confounded by the light, and fall an easy prey. They are killed for their oil and skins, which are considered of sufficient value to repay the risk of the adventure.

Murray's Handbook of Devon & Cornwall 1856

The eccentric poet parson Stephen Hawker recounted some engaging adventures in Boscastle, when he stayed at the former Ship Inn (centre right) in 1826. At that time a model of a local vessel swung above the door of the hostelry, and the ruddy faced, ample Joan Treworgy was the hostess.

When the Revd Stephen Hawker visited Boscastle with a fellow undergraduate in 1825, they were puzzled about the food they were given by the hostess of The Ship, who insisted that it was 'meat and taties'. Many years later he was horrified to read an ancient book which revealed that 'the sillie people of Bouscastle and Boussiney do catch in the summer seas divers young soyles (seals), which, doubtful if they be fish or flesh, conynge housewives will nevertheless roast, and do make thereof very savoury meat.'

Fetching water from the well in the nineteenth century.

In making and growth the soyle [seal] is not unlike a pigge, being ugly, faced and footed like a moldewarp (mole).

ANON.

Wrecks and Wrecking

The weather for ten days has been very awful and exceeding strange – thunder, hail, rain and storms of wind. The whole countryside is excited about these storms and the people connect them with the death of Mr ––, a merchant of Boscastle and a notorious wrecker.

Ten days agone a man called Jabez Brown living in Boscastle was returning at night when he saw sailing up the valley a cloud filled with bright fiery light. All the sailors saw it. It glided on over ——'s house and passed inland up the glen until it reached a church to which he belonged and where his family vault is.

On Sunday evening of this week —— went out on the cliffs and was watching the sea, it is supposed for wrecks. He returned quite well and went to bed. At five in the morning his servants heard him walk about the room. At six o'clock a vast roll of the tide came up the harbour and one of his vessels broke loose. The servants went in to tell him. They knocked: no answer. Again: silence. Frightened, they went in, and there he lay quite dead. His head was upon his hand. Ever since that day it is certain the storms have been continual, again and again with violence, and while I now write, my table trembles with the wind. All this is awful.

STEPHEN HAWKER 1858

Romance, drama, folklore, superstition, the capricious nature of the elements and the age old tradition of wrecking all come neatly together in this engaging letter. Stephen Hawker was a brilliant and eccentric poet parson, the vicar of Morwenstow, who befriended local characters like John Bray of Poughill, a former merchant, ship owner and salvage agent, gaining valuable insight into the harsh lives of eighteenth- and nineteenth-century fishermen, smugglers and wreckers.

Those were brutal times, and when shipwrecks occurred, excited bands of wreckers swarmed down to the shores to carry off anything they could get their hands on. To this impoverished community gleaning the bounty of the sea was part of the scheme of things. For just as the sea claimed its victims, it also yielded up its treasures, and they were grateful when it chose to do so on their shores. There were lurid tales of ruthless wreckers who lured vessels onto the rocks by the emplacement of false lights, murdering the survivors, and pillaging and plundering.

Shipwrecks were frequent occurrences, particularly in March and October, at the time of the Equinox. The age old tradition of wrecking was not confined to the lower orders of society. The right to wreckage was invested in the Crown, and lords of the manor and others of rank and power also established claims to the proceeds of shipwreck in their locality. By the nineteenth century it was customary for agents to make a rapid appearance on the scene to ward off wreckers and deal correctly with the salvage of the cargo. The proceeds from securing a contract were very lucrative, and at one time there was bitter rivalry between Mr Thomas Avery of Boscastle and Mr Shearm of Bude. On one occasion, when a vessel laden with hops was driven on shore near Kilkhampton in a heavy gale, the crew was helped to safety by local folk, with the aid of a rope. Whereupon a dispute arose between Mr Avery and Mr Shearm, with Mr Avery becoming very violent. This resulted in two law suits, which Mr Avery lost, as well as being compelled to pay thousands of pounds to the owners of the cargo.

If there was brutality by sea in former times, there was also the great humanitarian tradition of saving life from shipwreck, with ever vigilant watchers-on-the-shore, and heroic rescues by local fishermen. This area came to be covered by the establishment of lifeboat stations at Bude and Port Isaac. In October 1896, when the Danish barquentine Thyra was in distress, the Bude lifeboat was launched, and took off her crew of nine. As it was impossible for the lifeboat to return to Bude, the men landed at Boscastle, and the lifeboat had to be hauled back overland. The crew returned to their stricken ship, in the hopes of saving her by working the pumps. But unfortunately the vessel ran ashore and was wrecked on Dizzard Point, north of Crackington Haven.

Facing page: *Cottages known as 'Smugglers' and 'Tinkers' in Fore Street.*

This building, now known as the Harbour Lights, originally played a role in harbourside husbandry. The sagging roof, so characteristic of this area, results from unseasoned timber bending under the weight of the slates.

Smuggling and Piracy

Although this exposed shoreline, with its wild seas and high cliffs was an unfavourable environment for smuggling, it was the scene of some particularly bold and colourful exploits of the moonshine brigade. Manoeuvring small boats in and out of tight, rocky corners on dark nights called for the specialist skills of local fishermen, with an inbred knowledge of the dangers. Despite their slick technique, carefully positioned sunken rafts of contraband goods sometimes got broken up in the heavy seas, setting the precious kegs adrift. The steep and meandering harbourside at Boscastle was well suited for the concealment and inland movement of illicit goods, while terrifying tales of ghosts and witches and things that go bump in the night, served to keep inquisitive folk behind locked doors at crucial times.

This section of coast was patrolled by men of the Preventive Service, based here and at Bude. In the winter of 1820, when Chief Boatman Sampson Woodcock and his men were carrying out their duties in the Boscastle Preventive boat, they went ashore at Millook Haven and seized about 450 tubs of foreign rum spirits. As they were guarding their seizure, a fully rigged yellow, black and red smuggling cutter suddenly appeared on the scene, sent two armed boats ashore, and started firing at the beach. The officer and his men responded to the attack until their ammunition ran out. Whereupon the smugglers swarmed ashore, compelling them to retreat on account of being outnumbered. Having gained this advantage, the smugglers had the audacity to carry off the six-oared Preventive galley, as well as retrieving the contraband. Although the vessel must have been very conspicuous, the Commissioners of His Majesty's Customs at Padstow issued a description and offered a reward of £200 for information leading to the arrest of the miscreants. Sadly

the Boscastle boat capsized in a gale a few months later, and her crew of five was lost.

Of all the colourful characters associated with this seaboard, none achieved more notoriety than Crual Coppinger, the Dane, who arrived on these shores from a foreign rigged vessel during a devastating storm. The story goes that having emerged from the boiling foam, this fine and handsome figure of a man, who claimed to be highly connected in his homeland, snatched a cloak from an old woman's shoulders, flung it around his own, then leapt onto the back of a horse being ridden by a wealthy farmer's daughter, who had come down to the shore to witness the drama. The shipwrecked mariner was well received by the family, and married the lady when her father died shortly afterwards. However, the young bride soon discovered a darker side to his nature, and the situation got worse when their small son showed signs of being a chilling chip off the old block, bullying and blackmailing the local children.

The door to the Museum of Witchcraft, on the harbourside. This museum, set up in Boscastle in 1960, continues to intrigue visitors today.

Having gained wealth, Coppinger acquired a speedy vessel called the *Black Prince*, a motley crew of pirates, smugglers and press-ganged villains to crew her, and the reputation of being the terror of the seas. When it came to paying the price for a lengthy catalogue of wicked and dastardly deeds, Cruel Coppinger made his daring escape by sea, at the height of a dramatic storm. The lightning flashed and the thunder rolled as he boarded the vessel which awaited him. Then it seemed to fade away like a phantom ship, and folk slept more soundly in their beds thereafter.

The Willapark Lookout Tower was built near the remains of an Iron Age Fort.

Tourism

OCCUPATIONS IN BOSCASTLE:
Master mariner, excise officer, surgeon, solicitor, teacher, brewer, ironmonger, blacksmith, wheelwright, hemp and sand merchant, butcher, baker, brewer, maltster, tailor and shoemaker.

A Boscastle measure of Winchester bushels (Fig 7) and a Bodmin measure (Fig 8). Fig 7 was used as a water trough on the roadside near Barn Park in the late nineteenth century.

For centuries Boscastle was a close-knit, remote and rural community with its own culture. Superstition was rife and strangers were regarded with suspicion. Everyone knew everyone else's business, and the social life revolved around the churches, chapels, markets and festivals. Incidental daily interaction occurred around the school, shops, village wells and the harbour, as well as at the numerous public houses.

Few people travelled far beyond the village in those days, but the good communications indicate the importance of the Boscastle merchants. Horse-drawn vans ran from here to St Austell on Mondays and Fridays, and to Liskeard on Saturdays, returning the same day. Vans ran to Truro on Mondays, Thursdays and Fridays, and returned on Tuesdays, Fridays and Saturdays.

Farming was the main occupation, with the soil being described as 'dark loam, with a sub soil of rock and slate'. The chief crops were wheat, barley, oats and turnips, and the old guide books made mention of the early new potatoes. Life was hard and uncertain for those who worked on the land. If hired by the year, labourers received ten shillings a week, plus all the wheat needed for their families at twenty shillings a Camelford bushel (24 gallons), whatever the fluctuations in the retail price. If hired by the week, they were paid twelve shillings, but would be obliged to pay the market price for their wheat. The harbourside was the focus of this self-contained community, and the port provided employment for a wide range of skills. Folk often had large families, and food was not always plentiful, so it was customary for cottagers to grow their own vegetables and keep pigs and poultry, which were apt to wander around the

Boscastle Fair around 1905.

lanes. Fish was not a common commodity for local people, who consumed salted meat.

Life was tough, and itinerant travellers who passed this way in the hopes of gleaning a copper or two sometimes met a sad fate. In 1840, six vagrants, with organs and white mice, were committed from Boscastle to one month on the treadmill for begging by the Revd S. Chilcott. The following March an inquest was held in Boscastle on the body of an 86-year-old man, who had fallen and broken his thigh in a nearby lane, and lain there all night before being discovered. They took him into the town and sent for a surgeon, but he died shortly afterwards. Nobody knew who he really was, but he went under the name of Scotch Willy, and was in the habit of going around the countryside selling matches.

FACILITIES IN BOSCASTLE:

A Public Elementary School had been built in 1879, and by the 1920s there was a police station, a bank, a garage, refreshment rooms and many apartments and boarding houses. By the late 1930s the facilities had improved to include a private nursing home, a visiting optician and dentist, a newsagent, estate agent, confectioner, fruiterer, and shops selling fancy goods. There was a cycle agent, and car hire was also available.

The writer Walter White, who stayed at the *Commercial Hotel* in the 1850s, mentioned the well-appointed seats, allowing foot-weary walkers to enjoy delightful views across the harbour from the heights. These strategically placed seats had been emplaced by a public spirited inhabitant called Mr Fuggard, who had also excavated cliff cuttings and established walks for the enjoyment of the public at his own expense. On reaching the harbourside this traveller was enchanted to hear the smithy and his men rounding off a hard day's work with joyful and harmonious hymn singing.

The opening of Camelford Station in August 1893 was a turning point in Boscastle's fates and fortunes, for it siphoned off trade from the harbour, but also brought more tourists to the area. Horse-drawn buses and later motor cars and motor buses ran regular services to the station, which was 4½ miles away, and on the Launceston and Wadebridge section of the *London & South Western Railway* (later to become the *Southern Railway*).

The horse bus about to depart from the Wellington Hotel in July 1913. It was possible to get here by coach from Bodmin, Launceston and Bude at that time, and horse buses linked with the railway system at Camelford Station.

The advowson of the church of Forrabury anciently belonged to the de Boterell family, who subsequently granted this, with other possessions, to the Abbey of Hartland. Forrabury church remained vested in the Abbot and Convent of Hartland until the dissolution of the monasteries.

The parish of Forrabury, which is dedicated to St Symphorian, forms a conspicuous landmark from the sea. This saint, who was a native of Autun in Burgundy, was beheaded there in AD 178. The famous church, situated on the clifftops, high above the harbour, has attracted various colourful legends over the centuries. According to one, the Devil would not allow its builder to site it in a more accessible place, for fear of everyone being able to attend all the services. However, the most famous of these legends concerned its silent tower. It was said that when the church was built, the inhabitants, who had long been envious of the musical bells of neighbouring Tintagel, besought the Lord of Bottreaux to present them with a peal of bells as good as theirs. He duly ordered the bells, which were to be cast in London and delivered by sea. The subsequent disaster, in which the ship carrying the bells was sunk, is described on page 13.

Talkarn (Minster) Priory and Minster Parish Church

In ancient times there was a cell of the alien priory of St Sergius of Anjou in the romantic sylvan vale where the mother church of Boscastle now stands. It was founded by William Fitz Nicholas de Botreaux in the twelfth century, for the good of his soul and those of his ancestors. The monks were granted lands, tithes and other endowments. William de Botreaux, his grandson, confirmed this grant, but reserved for himself wood for fuel from the Prior's wood. If the monks should choose to use his mill, they could take priority over others who brought grist, rather than being obliged to await their turn. He also gave them rights of common pannage (pasture for swine and acorns and beech nuts as forage), common pasture (land with herbage for cattle), and turbary (the digging of turf or peat for fuel).

As with other cells of French priories established in England, its tenure was uncertain. In times of conflict with France, such priories might be seized by the Crown or very heavily taxed. Thus Talkarn experienced difficult times during the reigns of Edward I, II and III, when details of their profits, goods and chattels had to be declared. The priory seems to have ceased functioning about seven years before the dissolution of the monasteries in 1514–15.

Minster Church

Boscastle in the 1870s showing the Wellington Hotel as it was before the castellated tower was added.

Boscastle in 1894, by which time the Wellington Hotel had an embattled tower, the New Road to the right had been created, and Mr H.P. Lescallas had built some substantial split level houses on the hillslope alongside it.

The nineteenth century water mill adjacent to the Wellington Hotel in about 1930.

The Napoleon Inn in the High Street around 1905, when Mrs Grigg was the landlady.

The Napoleon Inn today.